Lumberjacks and Logging

COLORING BOOK

DRAWINGS BY

Chet
KOZLAK

Minnesota Historical Society • *St. Paul* • *1982*

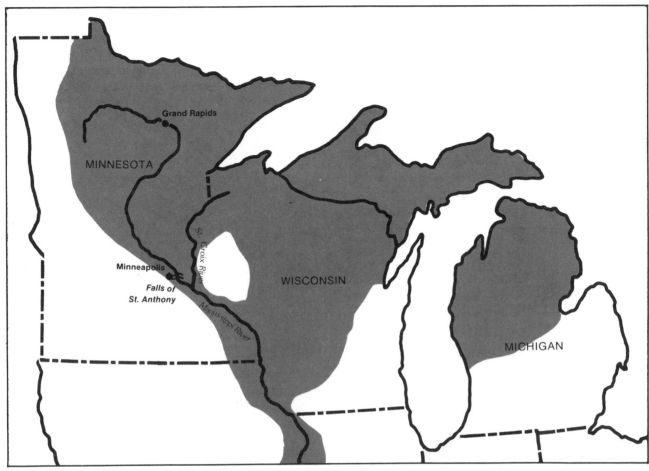

Location of the pine forests where lumbering companies were active in the 1800s and early 1900s.

INTRODUCTION

The lumbering business in America began in the early 1600s. Its first center was in New England. As the demand for lumber grew in the 1800s, the logging companies moved westward from Maine to Michigan and Wisconsin. By the 1830s Minnesota drew the lumbermen's attention because of the fine white-pine forests. The pictures in this book show logging and lumbering in Minnesota up to about 1900. This story is one part of a business that started along the Atlantic Coast and continues in the 1980s in the Pacific Northwest, the Upper Midwest, New England, and the southern states.

Minnesota land was chiefly of two kinds — prairie and forest. Most of the eastern half of the state was once covered with trees. The southeastern quarter contained hardwoods, such as oak, maple, and walnut. It was part of the Big Woods which reached westward from Michigan and Wisconsin.

In the area north and east of the Mississippi River (see map) the forest was mainly softwood — pine, fir, and spruce — as well as some hardwoods — mostly birch and maple. Early business in Minnesota centered on the wooded land. First, as part of the fur trade, men trapped the animals living in the forest. Second, the lumbermen moved in to cut the trees and float them down the many rivers to sawmills built near the growing towns. As early as 1837 lumberjacks from New England began cutting trees in the St. Croix Valley. Slowly the logging companies moved to the north and west until they reached the Canadian border.

The trees the lumbermen prized most were white pine, although other pine trees were also valuable. The white pine were very large, tall, and straight. One tree could produce several hundred feet of lumber. Farmers and townspeople building new homes in the midwestern states needed lumber for houses, barns, stores, churches, schools, and grain elevators.

Minnesota forests seemed to have enough white pine to meet all the demands for lumber.

Each fall logging companies hired crews of lumberjacks for the winter harvest. In spite of the cold, winter was the best time for cutting trees. Then the swamps were frozen, and trails could be made over the hard ground for dragging logs out of the forest. The companies set up camps. Each had a bunkhouse, a cookhouse with a dining room, a blacksmith shop, a company store or wanigan, and stables.

Life in the camps was hard. Six days a week the men woke to the call of "daylight in the swamp" and worked from "kin see" to "caint see." They ate typical frontier food — salt pork, baked beans, bread, flapjacks, molasses, doughnuts, dried-apple pie, and tea. After a quick breakfast, the crews headed into the woods. The undercutters notched the trees. The sawyers (men with saws) cut them down. The swampers trimmed off the branches before the sawyers divided the logs into regular lengths. A driver with a team of oxen or horses pulling a giant set of tongs or a sled called a go-devil skidded the logs out of the woods to the road. Then several loaders lifted logs onto a large sleigh and drove it to the nearest river. During the night an ice wagon poured water on the road leading from the piles of logs to the river.

The cookees (cook's helpers) carried a hot noon meal out to the loggers, who took a short break to eat. At sundown the crews returned to the camp and washed up. When the cookee sounded the bull horn, they trooped into the cookhouse. A good cook was necessary to a camp. Men might quit their jobs if the cook did not serve them delicious, well-cooked food. On most evenings in the bunkhouse the men played cards, read, or talked, but Saturday was special. The lumberjacks celebrated the end of the week with singing and dancing to fiddle or harmonica music.

Sunday was chore day when they did their laundry, wrote letters, and sewed up rips in clothing. Sometimes a traveling minister called a sky pilot offered church services.

With the arrival of spring the men's daily lives changed. The logs piled near the river had the owner's special brand stamped on each of them. The driving crews then rolled the logs into the water to float downstream. The first of three crews had to keep the logs moving. The second crew broke up log jams. The third crew picked up any logs that became stuck along the riverbank. A houseboat called a wanigan carried the kitchen and all supplies.

The river drive ended at the boom or collection point where each company sorted out its logs. Men who had memorized upwards of 2,000 log stamps hooked the logs and brought them into a floating corral belonging to their employer. Some companies sawed their logs at nearby sawmills. Rafting crews took others and roped several hundred logs at a time into rafts to be towed down the river to larger sawmills. The sawmills turned the logs into shingles and boards of many lengths. Trains then carried the lumber to the growing towns on the prairie.

Lumber companies and counties tried to sell the cutover land where the trees had once stood to settlers coming from Europe. In many areas the land was not good for farming. A farmer had to pull or blast out the stumps or plant around them and wait for them to rot. Rutabagas, turnips, potatoes, hay, and clover were the kinds of crops that grew successfully. Forest fires, which moved with alarming speed and often took many lives, were an ever-present danger for the farming families as they had been for lumberjacks and logging companies.

By 1920 most of the white pine in Minnesota had been cut down. The logging companies moved westward to Washington and Oregon and southward to Alabama and Georgia. The pine forest, an important natural resource, nearly vanished. Federal and state governments and members of the community began to co-operate in replanting pine trees. Today these trees are used for wood products (plywood), pulp (paper), and Christmas trees.

Although the day of the lumberjack has passed, it can be relived by visitors to the Minnesota Historical Society's Forest History Center at Grand Rapids. The center is a carefully rebuilt lumber camp. There are also exhibits explaining the lumber business.

These drawings by Chet Kozlak are based on pictures in the collections of the Minnesota Historical Society and on the reconstructed camp at the Forest History Center. The introduction and captions written by Sarah Rubinstein include information from many books on the lumber industry. The artist wishes to thank Robert (Skip) Drake, Marx Swanholm, Maureen Otwell, Bonnie Wilson, and Pat Harpole — all members of the Minnesota Historical Society staff; Floyd T. Ryan, former director of Keep Minnesota Green, and the Forestry Division, Minnesota Department of Natural Resources, for advice and assistance in the preparation of these drawings.

A forest ranger explains the way
a pine forest grows.

EASTERN WHITE PINE and RED (NORWAY) PINE

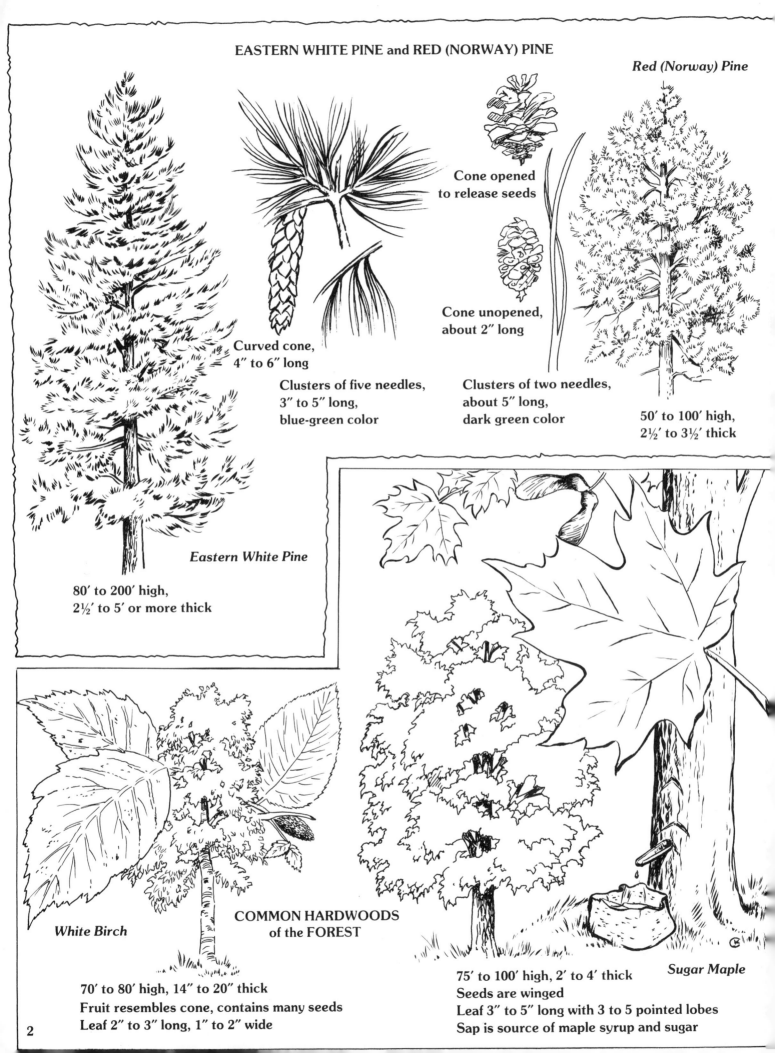

Red (Norway) Pine

Cone opened to release seeds

Cone unopened, about 2″ long

Curved cone, 4″ to 6″ long

Clusters of five needles, 3″ to 5″ long, blue-green color

Clusters of two needles, about 5″ long, dark green color

50′ to 100′ high, 2½′ to 3½′ thick

Eastern White Pine

80′ to 200′ high, 2½′ to 5′ or more thick

COMMON HARDWOODS of the FOREST

White Birch

70′ to 80′ high, 14″ to 20″ thick
Fruit resembles cone, contains many seeds
Leaf 2″ to 3″ long, 1″ to 2″ wide

75′ to 100′ high, 2′ to 4′ thick
Seeds are winged
Leaf 3″ to 5″ long with 3 to 5 pointed lobes
Sap is source of maple syrup and sugar

Sugar Maple

PAIL TUB & LUMBER MA ACTORY
PLANING MATCHING & PLITTING

Minnesota lumbermen first used the Falls of St. Anthony in the Mississippi River for power to drive their saws. The falls made Minneapolis an early center of the lumber industry in the state.

An undercutter swings an ax to cut a notch called a kerf. Next the tree is sawed through from the side opposite the kerf.

In the Forest

Two sawyers run as a giant white pine falls. Large splinters often shoot out from the cut edge.

Sawyers using a crosscut saw cut trees into logs. The branches the swampers trim off are left on the ground. When they have dried out they are a fire hazard.

A hot meal arrives on a sled called a swingdingle. Blankets packed around the pots keep the food warm.

A team of horses skids logs to the roadside.

As many as 50 logs could be loaded on a logging sleigh for the trip to the riverbank.

Water runs from holes in the ice wagon and freezes to form slippery tracks for the log sleighs to follow.

9

On a hill a road monkey spreads hay on the ice tracks to keep the sleigh from going too fast down the slope.

The Lumber Camp

Blacksmiths shoe horses and oxen and repair metal tools.

After a hard day's work, lumberjacks eat in the cookhouse. The cooks allow no talking, so there will be no fights.

In the evening lumberjacks relax in their bunks or sit near the warm stove. All wet clothing is hung up to dry.

"IT'S CROW WING RIVER FOR THE OLD PINE TREE"

Dancing, singing, and card tricks make Saturday nights lively. Some men wear aprons and pretend to be women dancing partners.

14

Scrubbing and boiling clothes clean and hanging them out to freeze dry is a regular Sunday chore.

A lumberjack buys a new shirt while the camp foreman or boss keeps track in the company books of the number of logs cut that day.

The River Drive

A scaler measures each log at the riverbank to see how many boards it will produce. The logs are already marked by stampers.

Log marks of some logging companies.

17

The drive to take logs down-river begins as soon as the ice goes out of the streams.

Pulling out the key log to break up a huge log jam is dangerous work.

This crew pushes the logs along to keep them moving. The wanigan floats down-river with the logs.

At the end of the drive, timber and chains form sorting booms to corral each company's logs.

One steamboat in the rear pushes and another in
the front rides crossways to steer a raft of lashed-
together logs down-river to the sawmills.

Logs move up a conveyor belt called a bull chain toward the steam-powered saws.

Lumber Milling and Uses

A train carrying cut lumber to build towns and farmsteads leaves the sawmill. A fire in the silolike burner gets rid of waste products.

Pine lumber found many uses from sidewalks to newspapers.

After the forests were logged off, farmers cleared the cutover land by dynamiting stumps.

Timberlands

Forest fires were a constant threat to people, wildlife, and trees — and they still are.

Today many people work together to replant forests for future use.